The
WALL STREET
Awakening

The Heart and Mind of Investing with Biblical Integrity

By

MARK A. MINNELLA, CFS, CFCA, CKA

XULON PRESS

Xulon Press
2301 Lucien Way #415
Maitland, FL 32751
407.339.4217
www.xulonpress.com

Printed in the United States of America.

ISBN-13: 978-1-54562-737-2

Table of Contents

Introduction

———— ❖ ————

"Iron sharpens iron and one man sharpens another."

Proverbs 27:17

*T*his book is divided into two main sections, the first section, "The Christians Investors' Devotional", was designed to give the reader Biblical concepts to consider in relationship to their investment philosophy, to prepare the heart. A chance to meet with God and explore possibilities. Possibilities that just might lead to a deeper relationship with the God of the Bible. Possibilities that might create a new way, or least an expansion to, how one looks at their investments.

Please take your time as you read through each of the daily devotionals to pause and consider. Give yourself the chance to digest, question, and then work and pray through each devotional. If you are one who journals, use the space to write down your thoughts and questions. If you like discussion, please go to www.BRIDevotional.

com and voice your thoughts, opinions and insights and engage with others doing the same.

The second section, "The Journey", was composed from the collective experiences and insights of this author's journey, over several decades, studying the Bible and applying the wisdom found there to investment practices. Where the first section is designed to engage and encourage you to form your biblical foundations, through a devotional approach, "The Journey" section was written more as an applicational handbook of Investing with Biblical Integrity.

A possible approach would be to consider reading through "The Christians Investors' Devotional" section to prepare the heart and then read through "The Journey" to develop your own personal Biblically Responsible Investment approach. No matter how you decide to use this book, my prayer is that you will be blessed through a greater understanding and appreciation of Investing with Biblical Integrity.

A Christian Investors' Devotional

> *"For what profit is it to a man if he gains the whole world, and lose his own soul? Or what will a man give in exchange for his soul?"*
>
> *Matthew 16:26*

———————————————

*F*ew would argue that the ultimate goal of investing is to gain additional wealth. But at what cost? What if a company you are currently invested in produced a product that was toxic to children? And what if because of that product your child is now deathly ill? Would you be comfortable being a partner in a company that is responsible for your child's pain? Would the possible gain in financial assets be worth the loss of your son?

What if a company you were thinking of buying stock in, becoming an owner, spent millions of dollars each year encouraging sexual immorality? And what if your daughter was now suffering with AIDs because she bought into such a lifestyle? Would the possible return on investment from owning stock in that company make up for the lifelong struggle your daughter now faces?

Every compromise we accept against God's sovereignty in this world compromises our relationship with our Father in heaven. What possibly could be worth limiting the fellowship we have with our Father who is the source of everything good and perfect? What value could there be that would be worth restricting the depth of our relationship with the one true God, the author of love itself?

"Behold, I send you out as sheep in the midst of wolves. Therefore be wise as serpents and harmless as doves."

Matthew 10:16

The Greek word for "wise" in this verse is the word "phronimos," meaning prudent, mindful of one's interest. The word "harmless" is the Greek word "akeraios," meaning without a mixture of evil, free from guile, innocent, simple.

If we are only as harmless as a dove, we may very well get eaten alive by the wolves of the world. If we are only as wise as a serpent, then we may end up hurting others. The key I find in these verses is to embrace both in our lives. We need the tools and wisdom to understand how money works, to develop a portfolio, to manage investments that correlate with our objectives, personality, and time horizons. This utilization of worldly knowledge and understanding of how money works is the "being wise as a serpent" part of the formula.

We also need to be aware of the impact our investments have in our lives and the lives of others. By being conscious of what we are participating in and supporting with our investment dollars we can choose the investment products that don't compromise our personal beliefs, that don't harm others. Utilizing care and compassion is the "being harmless as a dove" part of the formula.

What about in your life? Have you considered the Biblical wisdom of these verses regarding your investments?

"...And there is nothing new under the sun. Is there anything of which it may be said, "See, this is new"? It has already been in ancient times before us."

Ecclesiastes 1: 96 & 10

---

*T*hough the ability to capitalize a business receives the credit for the concept of incorporation, some believe that the formation of a corporation was originally instituted specifically to hide the activities of individuals behind the shield of a business entity. Corporate greed, at the expense of individuals and the morals of God, is nothing new. However, the ability to discern the activities, moral and deficient of morals, is relatively new.

With multiple channels of Cable airing news twenty-four hours a day, seven days a week, and the internet with Google, Yahoo, Wikipedia and so many more resources, it has become substantially easier to illuminate the dark secrets of corporations and individuals alike. Even if you find digging through the internet to be too much trouble, you can utilize one of the several internet services created specifically to do the research for you. One of the more popular subscription-based services for investment professionals is The Evalueator Services at www.Evalueator.com. For individual investors, www.mtmministries.org has a screening service that is free to individuals and comes with relevant and timely articles and information for the faith based investor.

The bottom line is, today it is not only possible to invest without compromising your Biblical values, it is easy. For some, this creates a crossroads of decisions. For others the decision is easy. If you are purposely trying to overlook the truth of what a company is promoting and profiting from, you may just find it harder to ignore. If, on the other hand, you believe that God is concerned with how, where, or what consequences your investments may produce, then you will be glad to know how convenient and easy it has become to invest with Biblical integrity.

"Love suffers long and is kind; love does not envy; love does not parade itself, is not puffed up; does not behave rudely, does not seek its own, is not provoked, thinks no evil; does not rejoice in iniquity, but rejoices in the truth; bears all things, believes all things, hopes all things, endures all things."

I Corinthians 13:4-7

---

*I*t is in the light of this guiding principle that John Calvin in his book "the Life of a Christian" instructs us on how to execute Biblical stewardship over "everything" bestowed upon us by God.

> "In regard to everything that God has bestowed upon us, and by which we can aid our neighbor, we are his stewards, and are

bound to give an account of our stewardship: moreover, that the only right mode of administration is that which is regulated by love."

—John Calvin, The Life of a Christian

Everything excludes nothing and includes investments. We are instructed to keep our investment activities within the guidelines of love, participating only in those things that do not provoke, act rudely, rejoice in iniquity, or think evil. We are to invest only in that which does not harm others or ourselves. His declaration was and is to manage (administer) our investments in and through the guidelines of love.

Have you ever considered the possibility that your investments, as well as providing for your future needs, could also be an act of love? How awesome is it that in every aspect of life, every activity we execute can and, if I read my Bible correctly, should be an expression of selfless love in this fallen world.

To bring this home and possibly help in the development of your own Faith Based Investing policies one might ask; "How could partnering with companies that use or abuse people ever reconcile with these tenets of love?"

"Test all things; hold fast what is good. Abstain from every form of evil."

1 Thessalonians 5:21-22

———————•———————

*S*ome have said that their lack of knowledge regarding the possible anti-biblical activities of the companies they own, either through mutual funds, directly in stocks, or through various other investment vehicles, insulates them from the impact of those decisions. But is it so? If one is purposely being ignorant of the consequences of their action, does that relieve them of their moral responsibility for the abuse, pain, death, and addictions that their investments might be profiting from and promoting?

We see in 1 Thessalonians 5:21-22 that it just isn't so. God calls us to test all things. "All things", not just some things. All things would include investments. We are to test our investments, hold on to that which is good and abstain from that which is evil. Is it possible He is calling us to be purposeful with our investment activities?

Calling us to realize a greater purpose, not at the expense of but along with the possible financial return on our investments?

Imagine a world where money flowed only to those companies that enacted business in a way that glorified God. Imagine an investment portfolio free from evil. Imagine a portfolio that has been purposely positioned to do well for financial needs and good for Godly means.

"Test all things; hold fast what is good. Abstain from every form of evil."

Have you tested your investments? Do you know what you might be holding on to?

"For the Lord your God will bless you just as He promised you, you shall lend to many nations, but you shall not borrow, ..."

Deuteronomy 15:6

———————•———————

What an incredible insight we can garner from these words. We see God telling Israel about the blessings they are to receive. The first "being a lender to many nations" and the second is that they will not be indebted to anyone.

It would seem from this verse that the act of buying bonds, lending money to a corporation, "may" be understood as participating in a blessing. I say "may", not because I am doubting God's word, but because God indicates the lending to be done is not to all nations thus indicating there are some they will not lend to. Why would He purposely exclude some entities from being lent to? One possible reason is because the all-knowing God of the

Bible might not want to fund entities, nations, that would use the money in ways that harm others and offend His tenants of love. To illustrate this one might ask whether it would make sense for a pro-life individual to knowingly purchase bonds (lend money to) issued by a company that financially supports abortion clinics? Or, what individual with strong convictions regarding the damage done by pornography and prostitution would purposely buy bonds in a company that produces pornography or a business that runs international prostitution houses?

Have you ever considered what type of companies God would be pleased with you buying bonds in, lending to, and what companies He would prefer His faithful stewards avoid?

"The earth is the Lord's, and all its fullness, the world and those who dwell therin."

Psalms 24:1

———————•———————

O ne of the foundational principles of Biblical stewardship, is the ownership of everything is the Lords. Everything including the earth itself. "Everything" excludes nothing and even includes you.

Before our saving relationship with God, we believed it was ours. Our cars, our houses, our retirement savings, our money, our boats and toys, ours…all ours.

Then God enters into our life and illuminates the truth that He alone is the creator and owner of everything in the world and that He entrusts what He may to us to manage to His glory.

Many good books have been written to explain the how's and what's of being a good and faithful steward, teaching us how God supplies us with resources for the caring of ourselves, our families and others and what it means to honor God with our finances. * What it means to be a steward of God's creation….. instead of an owner and the purposeful activities of honoring God with all He has entrusted to us…. including our investments.

What a privilege it is to be entrusted by the God of the universe with a portion of His wealth. Have you spoken to your Father in Heaven about His desires and direction for your investments? Be encouraged to take a moment to consider and pray about your investments as one of the many aspects of Biblical Stewardship. And may God bless you for doing so.

* One such book is "Money, Possessions, and Eternity" by Randy Alcorn

> *"Moreover it is required in stewards that one be found faithful."*
>
> *1 Corinthians 4:2*

---

*W*hat if someone had the heart and passion, mind and wherewithal to cure children with specific illnesses and builds a company specifically to do so? Over the years the company helps thousands of children realize a healthy and normal life free from disease. Then one day, the founder finds out one of his financial executives has been investing part of the company's profits in a company that has been found to promote and profit from products that actually harm children. If the founder's goals were truly first and foremost to help children, this employee would be found in rebellion to these goals and desires. Is there any doubt that this person lack of faithfulness to the owner's purposes would put them in direct conflict with the leadership that provided their livelihood?

From this perspective, shouldn't we consider whether God, the One whom everything we manage in our lives belongs to, would be comfortable financing the endeavor we may be investing in or lending His money to? This is one of those questions that is hard for some and easy for others. Mostly, due to what one believes about God and His word, the Bible.

"Do not be deceived: Evil company corrupts good habits."

I Corinthians 15:33

When I was a child my parents were very concerned with which kids I would hang with. They preferred certain friends over others. Even then, though I didn't want to admit it, I understood. It was the morally corrupt company I kept that introduced me to cigarettes, drinking, shoplifting and other immoral activities. These were not the good habits my parents taught me, but were the corrupted habits that I participated in, for a time, to be part of a certain group of kids. You know, the cool, tough, rebels. The same was true with the type of movies and television I wanted to watch. Despite what we may have said, and possibly continue to say, it does affect us.

First, we acclimate to something that would normally be offensive or shocking to our morals. Take for instant foul language. We are at first offended, then tolerable, and then finally find ourselves using the language that we found so offensive.

The same is true with our investments. Believe it or not there are companies that are in business to produce, promote and distribute Biblically offensive products and services and other businesses that use and abuse people, lie, cheat and steal, all to make a profit. If we try to ignore the possible offensive, immoral ways in which a company we invest in makes its profit, we may eventually find we are now acclimating to such activities. Activities, by the way, which we are now participating in through our ownership in that company.

Some would say they are more mature than a child and can stand against such influences against our character. My question then, to one who argues so, is if their character is so strong towards The Lord, why then would they own such a stock to begin with? Why would anyone who professes Christ want to partner with a company that outright insults their God by what it does or how it does it?

Please consider, that at the very least, the ownership of a stock is a financial endorsement of that company. By virtue of the law, stock ownership is the investor becoming an owner of the business and therefore partnering in all that the company does, good or bad.

So, what type of company are you keeping with your investments?

"And do not be conformed to this world, but be transformed by the renewing of your mind, that you may prove what is that good and acceptable and perfect will of God."

Romans 12:2

Conform

Made to resemble; assuming the same form; like; resembling.

Transform

Make a thorough or dramatic change in the form, appearance, or character of.

*P*aul gives us some wise direction here instructing us to not be like this world, thinking as they do.

For if one's logic and understanding is based on worldly foundations, then the conclusions and therefore the consequence of any action taken based on those thoughts will lead to a life that is worldly based rather than one that has a foundation in God's Kingdom.

We renew our minds by bathing our consciousness in God's Word, praying, and worship. The benefits of doing so are so great it would not do justice to try and communicate such in worldly terms. Yet it is so great, that it is worth trying.

Just imagine finding a peace that surpasses all understanding in your finances.

Imagine an investment portfolio that aligns your investments with Kingdom purposes. Imagine, because of the transformation of your mind, the peace, joy, freedom, and contentment that you could experience once you are no longer controlled by financial fears of this world but, are living according to God's eternal plan for your life.

"Awake to righteousness, and do not sin;..."

1 Corinthians 15:34

———————◦———————

*A*s a Christian, I am to be aware, awake, and conscious of what I do with my life and live it on purpose. Nowhere in the Bible does it tell us to bury our head in the sand or shut down our brain. In contrast, we are told to renew our brain, to awake to righteousness, to become aware, to be purposeful, and to expand our thoughts to include complex ideas like eternity and the spiritual world.

We are to awaken to righteousness and not sin. This means to be aware and purposeful in regards to what is right in God's eyes and then consciously take action to live accordingly in all aspects of our lives.

From a Christian investors perspective, is there any reason not to believe this directive should include being aware of the degree of righteousness, or the lack thereof, a corporation has in regards to how, what and why they

23

do what they do? If there is no exclusion for investments within this verse, what direction should a Christian, who has become conscious of immoral activities within companies they have invested in, take?

"You shall not bring the wages of a harlot or the price of a dog to the house of the Lord your God for any vowed offering, for both of these are an abomination to the Lord your God."

Deuteronomy 23:18

I have heard Christians proclaim that they invest for profit and profit alone. They then use the profits to help others and give to God. That it does not matter what they invest in but what they do with the profits. I applaud their desire to be generous and care for the poor, the widowed, and the hurting. Yet, if how they earn their money or what they invest in hurts others physically, financially or in any way, does a donation justify the pain?

This verse shows that God detests sin as well as any money derived from sinful activity. If this is true, do you think it matters to God how we invest His money?

"And have no fellowship with the unfruitful works of darkness, but rather expose them."

Ephesians 5:11

———————————•———————————

*T*here is no dancing around the meaning of this verse as it states clearly and with authority that we are to have nothing to do with the fruitless deeds of darkness. We are to reject, refuse and refute that which is of darkness. Darkness referring to evil, ungodly deeds. Darkness, such as harming others physically, mentally or emotionally (abortion, pornography). Darkness, like selfishly using others even to their demise, (pornography, prostitution, and immoral lifestyles). Preying on an individual's weakness and disease for personal profit with no concern regarding the ruin and destruction wrought. (Alcohol, tobacco, pornography)

It says have "nothing" to do..., nothing excludes every type of relationship, activity, or ownership including corporate ownership (stocks), partnerships, personal promises, lending to (bonds) or any other possible entanglement.

No, there is no getting around this directive from Paul to those of us who claim the name of Jesus. Please pray and consider the clear and concise message from Paul in light of your investments.

"Be anxious for nothing, but in everything by prayer and supplication, with thanksgiving, let your requests be made known to God; and the peace of God, which surpasses all understanding, will guard your hearts and minds through Christ Jesus."

Philippians 4:6-7

---

*T*he peace that surpasses all understanding…. wow. Wouldn't it be great just to walk continuously in that? Yet daily the distractions of this world and the pressures of life invade and overtake our state of mind. Politics, career, relationships, finances and so much more constantly and aggressively vie for our mind space and in the process, create frustration and anxiety in life. Interesting enough, it has been said that finances are the number one cause of marital arguments and the frustrations and anxiety of personal finance is the largest source of personal depression. Yet, our God says He will guard our hearts and minds if we turn to Him.

So why not turn to God and His word, the Bible, on how to manage, save, spend and invest his financial blessings? Imagine a life, by doing so, that actually begins to realize the peace that surpasses understanding. Please consider adding to your daily prayers gratitude for the wisdom and guidance that God provides you in your journey of becoming a Kingdom steward.

"Do not be unequally yoked together with unbelievers. For what fellowship has righteousness with lawlessness? And what communion has light with darkness?"

2 Corinthians 6:14

————————————————

What does it mean to be unequally yoked? In Biblical times a yoke was a wooden bar that joined two animals together to share the burden of plowing a field, pulling a cart, or some other burden. An "unequally yoked" team would have had one beast stronger or bigger than the other. The weaker would either have to walk faster to keep up or, more often than not, would walk slower than the bigger stronger one, pulling the load off track and increasing the burden to both animals. Instead of working together, they would be at odds with one another.

Today, the term "unequally yoked", is frequently applied to business and financial relationships. Why? Because unbelievers have worldviews and morals that often are in direct conflict with Biblical values. Values and personal beliefs guide decisions in life and business. Conflicting principals will naturally cause disagreement and eventually force one partner or the other to abandon their principals. Unfortunately, in today's world, the Christian is pressured to leave his Biblical principles behind for the sake of profit and the growth of the business.

Please consider that when you purchase stock, you are purchasing ownership in a company, you are becoming a partner with all the other stock owners. If you have little or no say, or are controlled by such an arrangement, have you become "unequally yoked"?

"But seek first the kingdom of God and His righteousness, and all these things shall be added to you."

Matthew 6:33

———————◆———————

God is looking to the fullness of our commitment to him not just a part of our relationship. He says "seek first the kingdom of God and all these things will be added to you".

As followers of Christ we need to ask ourselves whether we are seeking God first in all aspects of our lives. This would mean putting our faith in God, not in the ways of the world. It means trusting fully in God's wisdom not in the flawed and fallen ways of people, institutions or governments. It also means, when it comes to money, trusting in God's principles to guide us in how and what we do with our savings, giving, investments as well as all other aspects of our financial life.

In what ways have you allowed the world to butt in between you and God, to supersede God's direction as first in your life?

"Blessed is the man … Who walks
not in the counsel of the ungodly,
Nor stands in the path of sinners,
Nor sits in the seat of the scornful;"

Psalms 1:1

———————— ◆ ————————

"Blessed is the man"…..Oh how we desire the blessings of the Lord. To be in His favor, to bathe in His peace, joy and provision. Yet how often is it that we circumvent such blessings by compromising who we partner with, who we join in with? I am not saying we should avoid being in the world. Far from it. God's Word clearly tells us we are put here for a purpose. To be a light in the darkness, to profess Jesus as Lord and our salvation. But consider how walking in the ways of the ungodly circumvents not only our witness….. but possibly our blessings as well.

On another note, have you ever considered whether the counsel your investment advisor gives you ever steers you down the path of the ungodly? Even a little bit? Something to think about…or better yet, consider lifting your investment advisor and his or her investment counsel up to God in prayer.

"Therefore gird up the loins of your mind, be sober, and rest your hope fully upon the grace that is to be brought to you at the revelation of Jesus Christ; as obedient children, not conforming yourselves to the former lusts, as in your ignorance; but as He who called you is holy, you also be holy in all your conduct, because it is written, 'Be holy, for I am holy.'"

1 Peter 1:13-16

---

*I*nvesting with Biblical integrity can, for some, be a journey. The average Christian investor does not just wake up one day and realize the fullness of their actions.

Awareness, for some, comes slowly. For others, it can happen as one of those "ahha" moments.

Is it possible the more we desire God's will in our lives and pursue His holiness the more aware and conscious of His way we become? It seems from these verses it may be so. We can choose to purposely exercise the muscles of our mind to embrace God's way and not be controlled by the lusts and ignorance of our former self, the one without Christ. This applies to how we conduct every aspect of life including how we spend, save, invest and give of His financial blessings.

My prayer is that God would fill you with the mental strength and heartfelt desire to know His holiness in your life. Please take a moment to consider whether your investment portfolio conforms more to the lust and ignorance, as presented in 1 Peter 1:13-16, of your former self or to Holiness of our God.

"Who is wise and understanding among you? Let him show by good conduct that his works are done in the meekness of wisdom."

James 3:13

$\mathcal{H}$ave you ever watched someone who just had that presence about them? You know, they seemed strong and confident and yet made everyone around them feel comfortable. They were easy to be around. Strong, but not imposing. No one would consider them weak, yet they were gentle. And though they were vibrant, they had a quietness about them. Could this be what someone who conducts themselves in the "meekness of wisdom" looks like? Someone whose actions are gentle, peaceful, pure, and full of mercy, as is the wisdom of God.

Now consider someone who carefully and purposely chooses investments in companies of good conduct, where their products and services, those things that produce profits, are respectful, high quality and of high value. Companies that care as much about their clients, employees and vendors as they do about their profits. Companies that profit from or promote only that which does not compromise concepts of Biblical righteousness. Strong, vibrant, profitable companies that execute business with honor.

Could this be what a wise and understanding investor who conducts themselves in the "meekness of wisdom" looks like?

"But if you have bitter envy and self-seeking in your hearts, do not boast and lie against the truth. This wisdom does not descend from above, but is earthly, sensual, demonic. For where envy and self-seeking exist, confusion and every evil thing are there."

James 3:14-16

---

*M*aking money is not evil. Having an IRA or retirement account that produces a good return is not demonic. It is the state of our heart regarding these assets that is being considered here. And the heart issue is what guides one's investment decisions.

Is it possible that we might compromise Biblical values if pride is the motivator of our investment choices?

Could we possibly ignore the evil a company may perpetuate if greed dominates the decision process?

The good news is that investing can exist outside the darkness of greed and pridefulness. Investing with Biblical integrity takes in the full counsel of God to consider the what, how and why one is investing. It aligns the objectives as well as the execution of investment choices with Gods directives of love. It takes the "self-seeking" out of the process, so that all decisions can be based on wisdom from above.

If you have investments, take a moment to give thanks for the abundance. He has trusted you with much. Also, please pray that all pride and greed would be removed from your heart regarding these investments. Finally ask God to guide the what, how and why of your investment decisions. In doing so, I pray that you would realize the joy of the Lord that comes from being a good and faithful steward.

"But the wisdom that is from above is first pure, then peaceable, gentle, willing to yield, full of mercy and good fruits, without partiality and without hypocrisy."

James 3:17

———————————◆———————————

*D*id you ever wonder how to discern the wisdom of God? What would it look like? What differentiates it from the so-called wisdom of the world? Well wonder no more, James has given us some descriptive characteristics of Godly wisdom in this verse.

Someone once said wisdom is the conduit that guides good decisions, Godly wisdom is the vehicle that drives God honoring great decisions. Consider how weighing all matters against these characteristics could impact your life in Christ. What a great filter and guide to help walk in the ways of our God and Savior.

Now consider the positive impact your investment decisions could have if the activities, products, services, management and donations of the companies being considered as possible investments were weighed against the characteristics of Godly wisdom.

"See that no one renders evil for evil to anyone, but always pursue what is good both for yourselves and for all."

I Thessalonians 5:15

———————•———————

*P*ursue what is good both for yourselves and for all. Pursue means to hunt, to hound, and search for. It implies actively, even passionately, going after something. That something here is "what is good for yourself and others". We are encouraged and instructed to make doing good a passion. And doing so in contrast to doing evil to anyone.

Investing with a Biblically responsible approach has the unique ability to fulfill doing what is good for "yourselves and for all". First, your money can be put to work on achieving your personal financial objectives such as creating a secure and comfortable future for yourself, caring for and educating your family, and all important financial objectives you may have. Second, by purposely using only investment products that are in alignment with your Biblical values, you avoid rendering evil to anyone and only pursue doing good for all. Investing with Biblical integrity helps your money perform both tasks without compromise.

"A faithful man will abound with blessings, But he who hastens to be rich will not go unpunished."

Proverbs 28:20

---

*A*n interesting contrast is presented here. One between being a faithful man and that of one who hastens to be rich. It seems the word "hastens" plays a big part in this comparison. Often this word is used to denote the speed of actions, specifically a faster, immediate response. This may apply here as well, but there may be much more to it, especially in context with the contrasting word faithful.

To be faithful one would be purposeful, conscious, deliberate in their pursuit, in this case, of honoring God. In contrast one who hastens to be rich might neglect any and all cautions and Godly principles, hastily ignoring the eternal values that might complicate or confuse the singular short-term objective of material wealth.

God does not say we must choose between temporal wealth and eternal riches. He says we are to choose which we will serve. Will we be faithful to God's path for our life? A life that embraces both the physical, this temporal moment we call life, as well as the spiritual, life eternal. Or will we serve only the material, temporal god of riches?

The same is true regarding investments. Few would argue that the intent of investing is the increase of wealth. Again, God does not say to forsake temporal prosperity, but to be faithful to Him and His perfect desires for you, now and for eternity, in all things, including the activities of investing. What a wonderful, powerful realization it is that we can invest for the here and now, for real world results, and stay faithful to God's eternal significance when His word, the Bible, is the foundation and center of our actions.

Though it might be a bit scary to do so, please consider asking God where you could be even more purposeful, conscious, and deliberate in your pursuit of honoring Him?

"The land is Mine, for you are strangers and sojourners...."
"The silver is Mine, and the gold is Mine, says the Lord of hosts."

Leviticus 25:23; Haggai 2:8

❖

The foundation of Biblical Stewardship is the knowledge of and acceptance that everything is God's. He is the creator, ruler, and power that keeps it in existence. God owns it all.

We, on the other hand, are given stewardship over all that He sees fit to entrust to each of us. God created us to be good and faithful stewards. Being a Christian means one has accepted the truth that Jesus redeemed their life with His. Biblical Stewardship is the term giving to how a Christian should live out that truth in relationship to this temporal and material world. The question is not whether one should be a steward or not but rather what type of Steward one will be. Everything in creation is

God's including you and me. He created us and bought us with a price.

Bottom line, Biblical Stewardship is the use of God's resources, which is everything including time, talents and treasure, to accomplish God's purpose executed in a manner that Honors and Glorifies our God and Savior. Please consider how the concept of Biblical stewardship applies to the blessings God has entrusted to your management. This would, of course, include your investments.

"For by Him all things were created that are in heaven and that are on earth, visible and invisible, whether thrones or dominions or principalities or powers. All things were created through Him and for Him."

Colossians 1:16

———————❖———————

*T*ry to picture an altar of worship. On that altar is everything in life that God has entrusted to you, which would mean everything in your life would be there. Now what on that alter would you like to remove and not give to God, not offer up as an act of worship?

Some might say their sin or burdens. Yet that is why Jesus came, to pay for our sins, to lighten our burdens. He wants us to trust Him, an act of worship, by surrendering the burden of our sins to him. Another way to look at this would be to ask why would anyone, who truly loves the Lord, want to limit their ability, options, and the ways in which they could worship God, by removing anything from that altar.

Could the problem be our perspective? Many believers in Christ see their lives, and everything in it, as this mess to sort through and pick through to try and find something righteous and pure to place on that altar of worship. Things that are worthy. My friend, in and of itself, there is nothing we do that is pure enough or worthy enough to earn a place on that altar of worship. Yet, in Christ, there is nothing in and about our lives that has not already been accepted.

One of the saddest matters I have observed in a Christian's life is when one categorizes money, or anything else for that matter, as nothing more than a temporal and material concept, something that does not have a spiritual aspect to it. Something unworthy to participate in the worship of God. When this happens, the outcome at best is that money and finance become a distraction to one's relationship and intimacy with God. Or worse, becomes an idol or addiction. Something that separates us, at least a part of ourselves from God. Yet we see in God's word that all things were created by God for His glory.

When we are born again we are born of the spirit. We now are both physical and spiritual. Living in the temporal and eternity. There is no segregating the two. We are to honor God with all we have and are. Not admitting that our money and investment are part of everything is like taking things that God has already accepted, off the altar of worship to our Savior.

How awesome it truly is to realize every aspect of our life can be included in the worship of our Lord and Savior, including, what and how we invest. Please consider how investing can be so much more than just money. Investing, like every aspect of our lives can, and I would submit, should be an act of worship.

*"For where your treasure is, there
your heart will be also."*

Matthew 6:21

A well know verse for sure. Randy Alcorn in his
book "The Treasure Principle: Discovering the
Secret of Joyful Giving" explains;

"By telling us that our hearts follow our treasure,
Jesus is saying, "Show me your checkbook, your VISA
statement, and your receipts, and I'll show you where
your heart is." Suppose you buy shares of General
Motors. What happens? Suddenly you develop interest
in GM. You check the financial pages. You see a magazine article about GM and read every word, even
though a month ago you would have passed right over
it. Suppose you're giving money to help African children with AIDS. When you see an article on the sub-
ject, you're hooked. If you're sending money to plant
churches in India and an earthquake hits India, you
watch the news and fervently pray. As surely as the

compass needle follows north, your heart will follow your treasure. Money leads; hearts follow." [1]

What if, instead of money, our treasure truly is in Christ? Does that mean we no longer care about the present? Considering that God himself created heaven and earth, even time itself, and then inserted us into this creation, indicates that God cares about the here and now. Since He cares, shouldn't we?

Our hearts should be with God. This does not negate the importance of the here and now. It should however guide our decision process, navigate our steps and define our choices. It would focus us on whatever will bring us closer to our treasure. And that is a good thing.

So, if one's treasure was a complete and perfect relationship with God, in what ways do you think that your heart for God would guide investment decisions differently than if one's treasure was elsewhere?

---

[1] Pages 43-44 The Treasure Principle: Discovering the Secret of Joyful Giving by Randy Alcorn

"Let him turn away from evil and do good; Let him seek peace and pursue it."

1 Peter 3:11

———————◦———————

*T*hese words are quoted from the Old Testament by Peter as he concludes his instructions on living a Godly life to the believers of his time. He uses wisdom here that is timeless. Wisdom that was given in times past, was true in his day, and applies to us now. It is clear and sound in its message, "turn away from evil and do good." When we become aware of evil we are to turn away from it. Reject it. Have nothing to do with it. Evil as in those things that offend God. Evil such as using or abusing God's children. Evil such as the act of murder, brutality, and sexual immorality, or the promotion of such things. Without compromise, we are instructed to turn away from everything evil and choose the joyfulness of God's better way of pursuing peace. With others…. with God.

Please take a moment to reflect on each aspect of your life in light of this verse. Work, play, relationships…. even worship. Are there tumors of evil that need rejection? Pray for the wisdom to identify, and the strength to reject, all forms of evil so that you may feel the complete joy of the Lord and the peace that surpasses all understanding.

Have you ever considered what evil may be present in your investments as well? It is possible to know. Here are a few of free resources for your consideration.

<u>More Than Money Ministries</u> – A nonprofit organization with a special focus on Investment Stewardship. They provide free screening, educational articles, videos and community for those interested in investing with Biblical integrity. <u>www.mtmministries.org</u>

<u>Evaluator Services</u> – A Biblically Responsible data provider for investment professionals, will screen your portfolio for you for free, no strings attached. <u>www.evalueator.com</u>

<u>The National Association of Christian Financial Consultants (NACFC)</u> – The first organization formed to teach, train and encourage Christian financial professionals to provide Biblical Stewardship, including "Biblical Responsible Investing to their clients." <u>www.nacfc.org</u>

<u>Kingdom Advisors</u> – Kingdom Advisors provides advocacy, training, and community for financial professionals who are specialists in offering Biblically wise advice. <u>www.kingdomavdisors.com</u>

"See then that you walk circumspectly, not as fools but as wise, redeeming the time, because the days are evil. Therefore do not be unwise, but understand what the will of the Lord is."

Ephesians 5:15-17

---

*J*ust as wisdom is needed to minimize risk and maximize return in your investments, wisdom is needed to maximize one's life in general. Specifically, Godly wisdom.

Here we see that we are encouraged to avoid the foolishness of taking the lazy way out and instructed to be wise, to redeem the time. To understand the will of the Lord is to be wise. The understanding of God's will comes by purposely pursuing Him through study, prayer and practice. Imagine a life where every opportunity to know and align our life with God is realized. What would that look like in the way we work? How would that play out in what we do with leisure time God provides? What joy might we feel in each decision we make when we have purposely evaluated the options and choose that which is founded in Godly wisdom?

Please consider the opportunity to exercise Godly wisdom in your investment choices. Choices that avoid the "evil" of these days. Choices that align with what the will of the Lord is. Ask God to help you redeem every aspect of your life for that which is good, righteous, holy, and profitable.

"Therefore, whether you eat or drink or whatever you do, do all for the glory of God."

1 Corinthians 10:31

———————— ⁝ ————————

*M*y experience with Christians is that somewhere in them is the desire to honor God in all they do. Even baby Christians feel this desire as they begin their struggle, with letting go of worldly desires, to embrace the eternal significance of their life. Though it is a journey, one that takes a lifetime, the heart of it all is the pursuit of honoring God, in all we do.

Even in the basics of life, such as what we eat or drink. We can by His strength and power, become conscious of our decisions and strive to make our life journey an act of love, thereby honoring God purposely with every breath we take, every move we make.

Have you considered what diverse opportunities, God has provided for you, to participate more fully in His grace, glory, and joy by simply choosing to honor Him in "whatever you do"… including your investments?

"Therefore, to him who knows to do good and does not do it, to him it is sin."

James 4:17

———————•:•———————

*P*lease pray over this verse and consider your next steps regarding the investments God has entrusted to you. Write in the space below what you believe God would like you to do.

God's directions for my investments:

1. _____
   _____
   _____
   _____
   _____

2. _____
   _____
   _____

_____
_____

3. _____
_____
_____
_____
_____

4. _____
_____
_____
_____
_____

The Journey

The Journey

---※---

*A*s founder and President of Integrity Investors, I have spent the better part of my life in the investment and financial industry. During those years I have been fortunate to participate in the establishment and rise of a movement in Christianity to incorporate Biblical values into the investing arena, best known today as the Biblically Responsible Investment movement. In answering God's call to do so, I have been blessed to work with many great Christian business people. It has always amazed me that God would allow me to sit at the tables of such great people, even serve with them. But that is how God works. Sometimes he uses the foolish, read me, and the weak, again….me, to show His power.

Three such men of mighty valor are Art Ally, the founder of the Timothy Plan Mutual Funds, Glenn Repple, the founder of G.A. Repple and Company, and Mick Owens, the founder of CFD Investment, Inc. All three totally sold out to the service of the Lord and each completely unique in personality and their approach to the development of the movement.

It was in the early 1990's that God seemed to strike the heart of the four of us, and others, with the mission of revealing Christ on Wall street. Somehow, in His power and majesty, God brought us together with one singular focus. That focus was to bring awareness to the world of God's stewardship designs for investments, as revealed in His word, the Bible.

Art formed the Timothy Plan mutual funds, the first mutual fund openly and by prospectus to screen for Biblical principles. Glenn transformed his brokerage services into the premier Christian investment firm in America. Mick developed and made Biblical foundations the anchor of the financial planning systems at CFD, the brokerage and financial planning service firm he founded. A separate book could, and should, be written about the journey of each of these men and the influence and wisdom that formed the foundations for today's Christian investment services and investor awareness. It would not be too much to say that any and every Biblically based investment service today was built on the backs of these men.

It was shortly after Art had founded the Timothy Plan Mutual Funds that we came together to form the National Association of Christian Financial Consultants, NACFC. The sole purpose was to educate and equip Christian investment professionals in the wisdom and application of Biblically Responsible Investing, known then as

Values Based Investing and Faith Based Investing. Our first meetings were more like Bible studies and worship meetings, than business meetings, as we struggled individually and corporately to understand God's directives for the Christian investor. We shared, discussed, and yes, even argued about these concepts. And we prayed. We then began reaching out to the investment community to bring together those who knew that God had so much more than commerce in mind for them. It was a slow, hard journey with attacks coming from both outside and inside the Christian community. Yet slowly the movement took legs and God's word stood firm.

What I have come to discover about this journey, is the reality of a similar process. The process of discovery and embracement that many believers travel themselves, emotionally and spiritually, in realizing God's desire for their investments. I would like to share with you some investment insights gleaned over the years of my Investing with Biblical Integrity journey.

Personal Values

A wise Christian once told me that everything we do, every action we take is either an act of worship.... or an act of rebellion towards our God and Savior. Over the years, I have found this to be true and believe if you think about it and boil it down for yourself, you too will find that most, if not all actions can be sorted into those two camps. Including our investments. Let me explain by first asking a question.

Did you ever meet someone who said one thing and did another? At best, it was very confusing. It was obvious that what they communicated with their words was clearly in conflict with what they communicated with their actions. Today, more than ever before, there seems to be less continuity between what most people say and what they do. The virtue of truth does not seem to be a core value the bulk of our society embrace.

Maybe you have seen some of the polls of college students where the majority admits they would cheat to pass a test or the college graduates that confess they would or have lied to get a job or advance their career. To a Christian, this seems to fly in the face of everything we believe to be right. Yet, a large portion of those polled claimed to be Christians. So, what is happening?

As our world continues to promote the values of "success", worldly success, as defined by how much money and power you have, we see more and more individuals embracing this temporal concept and the attainment thereof as their core value, their most precious treasure. The value of money then becomes more important than truth and the chasm between what is said and what is done grows ever wider.

Ultimately, it comes down to personal values. We all have our own set of personal values, and these personal values guide our actions. Sure, no two people share identical sets of values, but for most Christians there is a wide expansion of common ground. Christian values are based on our faith in Jesus Christ and God's written word, the Bible. When making decisions in this life it is this value set, our beliefs based in God's love, that guide our actions.

I remember an experiment I observed when I was in college. The instructor explained this was an experiment in sensory perception and that a blindfolded participant would be exposed to different physical sensation. He then would be asked to identify what it was. A volunteer was solicited, let's call him Greg, blindfolded and seated next to the professor in front of the class with his hand and arm laying palm up on the desk. The Professor then pulled a tissue out the tissue box on his desk and gently rubbed it against Greg's' forearm and asked him what he thought it was. With confidence, Greg proclaimed it to be a Kleenex. When asked how he could be so sure he admitted seeing the Kleenex box on the desk and hearing the professor pull it out and finally feeling it on his arm.

With the student still blindfolded the professor noisily opened a box of match sticks, pulled one from the box, struck it on the side of the box and held up the lit match for all to see. Even in the back of the room I clearly heard the unique scraping sound a match makes as it is struck and there could be no mistaking the smell of sulfur burning as the match burst into flame. No doubt the blindfolded participant was acutely aware of what was happening as well.

Without missing a beat, the professor silently placed the match in an ashtray, grabbed an ice cube from underneath his desk and touched it directly on Greg's arm. Instantly Greg screamed and jerked his arm violently away from the desk. As he whipped his blindfold from his face he began yelling at the professor about being so irresponsible and burning him. It was a good half minute before he realized the professor was holding an ice cube, not a lit match. Greg's eyes shot back and forth between his arm and the ice cube several times before he finally adjusted to the fact that he had not been burned. Greg fully believed the professor had placed a lit match on his forearm….. and acted accordingly.

This example clearly demonstrates that we all act according to what we believe. The same is true in everyday life. If we believe something to be dangerous, we take precautions. If we believe something to be safe, we are at ease with the handling of or experiencing what an item or situation will bring. It is our set of values and beliefs that influence our decisions and determine our actions. Why should it be any different regarding investments decisions and actions, the most common of which is the buying and selling of stock?

The Stock Connection

---❖---

Corporation, n., An ingenious device for obtaining profit without individual responsibility.

Ambrose Bierce

Participation

The term "stock" is short for "stock certificate". It refers to the document used as evidence or proof of ownership in a corporation.

For a Christian, it is essential to understand that owning stock means you are an owner of a company. The more stock you own the larger your ownership of that corporation. As an owner you participate in the profits made from the activities of the company. You also have certain rights such as are represented by the type and amount of stock you own. Voting rights, or the influence regarding leadership and control of the company, are a couple of the more common rights. Because you are an owner/participator in the profits you also are an indirect participator in the activities of the company.

When you buy stock, you are effectively partnering with all the other stock owners in that company. Though you may not be held directly responsible for the actions of the company as a minority stockholder, you are a participant just the same. Let's say for ease of math you own 10% of company XYZ's stock. If that company creates a cure for some terrible disease you have the pleasure of knowing the company, you have become a partial owner in created that cure. If you were sole owner, owning 100% of the company's stock, you would be credited personally for making such a great breakthrough and would reap the rewards of the possible profits from the patents, rights, and sales of this great product. As 10% owner you participate in the possible increase of the value of your stock and may receive dividends from the profits proportionately to your ownership in such breakthrough.

The same unfortunately is true on the other side of the formula. If the company you own creates, distributes, markets, and or promotes products or services that harm others and are clearly offensive to Christian Biblical values, then you have the unfortunate privilege of participating in these activities through your stock ownership in that company. Some such products or services that most

Christians would agree violate God's basis of love, that harm or abuse His children, include:

- Pornography and Prostitution – The use and abuse of individuals for sexual activities.

- Abortion-Ending an infant's life.

- Addictive products-The production and promotion of products, that harm even destroy the consumer.

- Anti-Christian, anti-God, entertainment and publication that promote, desensitize and program our society to reject God and the Bible.

- The promotion of Immoral Lifestyles that reject the Biblical principles of marriage and sexual relations.

When we own stock in a company that develops, distributes or promotes such products or services we become a passive participant in that Biblically offensive activity.

To illustrate this point more clearly let's pretend there was a company that made 100% per year return for its stock owners. Most people would love to have an investment portfolio full of such stocks. But what if this company made such good returns from the production of child pornography and prostitution activities in third world nations. Do you think most Christians would feel different about participating in such profits?

Some stock owners may argue that they did not exploit and destroy the children's lives enslaved to prostitution and pornography. They just invested in a company. Yet by buying the stock an investor has financially shown support for the activities, endorsed with their money the services and have profited directly from the abuse of these children. A stock owner may be a passive participant but a participant just the same.

To maintain integrity between our core beliefs in our God and our investment actions we need to know with clarity what we truly believe, have a strong grip around our faith and then be conscious of what we are participating in when we invest in stocks.

Larry Burkett once wrote "We need to be careful about what our investment dollars are supporting. Some companies that typically offer strong profits prey on the weaknesses of others – gambling enterprises are a good example. Christians need to think twice about investing in any company that would be deemed socially unethical. My advice is to stay away from any company that makes money from activities that are morally reprehensible." [2]

---

[2]   Larry Burkett, Sept, 2002 Money Matters Newsletter

The good news is many companies do not participate in such items or services. Yet we must still be careful.

Corporate Charity

A company can do many things with the profits it generates from its business activities. Profits could be used to expand the business, develop new products and be distributed to the stockholders in the form of dividends. A corporation, just like an individual, can also make charitable gifts of its cash flows, giving financial support to organizations the controlling stockholders believe are worthy.

Most corporate donations do not go through a democratic vote of all the stock owners to decide what, if any, social and charity activities to fund. It is often decided by a few people of influence within the company, usually the officers and directors. Remember, a corporation can have millions of owners. The idea that 6 to 12 directors can decide to take profits from millions of stockholders and fund their personal agendas through corporate donations seems very wrong to many investors. Especially when those "causes" being supported are in direct conflict to the values of many stockholders.

Imagine a profitable company deriving millions of dollars in profits from the manufacturing and distribution of healthy, tasty baby foods. If you owned stock in this company, you would hope the profits would be distributed to you and to the many other stockholders. But what if instead of distributing profits, that company took a portion of those profits and donated them to Planned Parenthood, America's number one abortion provider?

Some stock owners might argue that they didn't make the donations themselves or even agree with the decision to give to that organization, so they are not responsible for any harm done by such actions. Yet, by buying the stock, or holding on to it after such decisions have been made, an investor has shown acceptance for the leadership and have endorsed, with their ownership, the decision to donate to such organizations. Remember, even if a stock owner is a passive participant, they are participant just the same. The Biblically Responsible Investor considers both how a company generates its income, as well as what it does with the profits.

On another note, you may be thinking this illustration is pretty far-fetched. Surely, no company would donate to an organization that kills its potential clients. I wish it were so, but unfortunately this illustration is based on a true story.

The Bond Connection

———————— ❖ ————————

Lending to Corporations

*W*hat about bonds? Just like stocks, it is essential to understand what "bonds" are so we can fully understand how they may play a role in the faith based investing process and where they may cause compromise. A bond or debenture is a debt instrument. It is essentially an I.O.U. or promissory note, evidence of a debt from the issuer, usually a corporation or government entity, to the purchaser who is known as the bondholder. A bond is usually offered or sold in multiples of $1,000 and $5,000, though other denominations have existed. The bottom line - A bond is a contract to pay the bondholder a specified amount of interest over a predetermined time frame and then to pay back the original loan amount, known as the "face amount", at the end of that time. It is not ownership in a company but lending to that entity. The bond purchaser becomes the lender. This is an alternative way of raising funds for a corporation in lieu of selling stock. It allows the current stockholders to raise capital without having to sell all or a portion of their ownership in the company.

Ok, so a bond is essentially you lending money to a corporation or government entity. Now how does that fit with the Biblical principles of investing with Biblical Integrity? Interestingly the Bible tells us in Deuteronomy that lending is a blessing, as compared to borrowing being a curse.

Deuteronomy 15:6 (NKJV) "For the Lord your God will bless you just as He promised you, you shall lend to many nations, but you shall not borrow, ..."

Deuteronomy 28:12 (NKJV) " The Lord will open to you His good treasure, the heavens, to give the rain to your land in its season, and to bless all the work of your hand. You shall lend to many nations, but you shall not borrow.

Deuteronomy 28:43-45(NKJV) The alien who is among you shall rise higher and higher above you, and you shall come down lower and lower. He shall lend to you, but you shall not lend to him, he shall be the head, and you shall be the tail. Moreover, all these curses shall come upon you and pursue and overtake you, until you are destroyed, because you did not obey the voice of the Lord your God....

Funding the Enemy

Borrowing equals curse…lending equates to blessings. So, if someone is purchasing bonds, lending money to a corporation, then they "may" be participating in a blessing. I say "may" because the same concepts of stewardship apply to bonds as they do stocks. Let me give you an example in the form of an imaginary letter written from a fox hole in Iraq.

Dear Sally,

I miss you and the kids so much. It seems like it has been forever since I have been home and I have seen so much blood, pain and destruction. I lost both of my best friends in a battle just this last week. Remember Bob? He is on his way home, lucky guy, though I don't know if his leg will ever heal right. But on another note the enemy doesn't seem to be able to replace equipment or keep supplied. I believe they are running out of money to finance their war against us. Recently I saw they were issuing bonds to raise money to fight us. They are promising to pay huge interest. Hey maybe we should loan them the money. Sure they are the enemy and it may advance their cause..even cause us to be captured and defeated or worse… killed, but think of the return….

Can you imagine any American soldier writing home to his wife such a letter? Of course not. No one in their right mind would go to war with and simultaneously finance their enemy. The same is true in investing. What kind of insanity would have to exist for a pro-life individual to knowingly purchase bonds issued by a company that supports abortion clinics? Or what individual with strong convictions regarding the damage done by pornography and prostitution would purposely buy bonds in a company that produces pornography or a business that runs international prostitution houses? It just would not make sense. If a Christian investor has the knowledge of what they are supporting, participating in, or profiting from then such investments would become ugly and distasteful, a compromise of that we hold most precious...our relationship with and the honoring of our God and Savior.

The Steward's Perspective

Another way to look at it, another possibility, emerges if we accept the Biblical principle of being a steward of all we have instead of an owner. The foundation of which is God's ownership over everything.

> Psalms 24:1 The earth is the Lord's and all its fullness, the world, and all who dwell therein.

Leviticus 25:23 The land is Mine and you are strangers and sojourners with Me.

Haggai 2:8 The silver is Mine, and the gold is Mine, says the Lord of hosts.

1 Corinthians 4:2 Moreover it is required in stewards that one be found faithful.

This concept is one most Christians agree with, but few live by. A good and faithful steward is to manage Gods resources, God's way, for God's purposes. So, let's break this down.

First, if God owns everything, he owns the investments we are discussing. Second, if we are to manage God's resources, stewardship would dictate it be managed as an act of love. Love is His way. Finally, it would be managed to His glory, His purposes. From a Biblical Stewardship perspective, shouldn't we at the very least, consider whether God, the one everything we manage in our life belongs to, would be comfortable financing the endeavor we are considering lending (buying bonds), His money too?

A Short History of Investing with Biblical Integrity

──────────◆──────────

"…And there is nothing new under the sun. Is there anything of which it may be said, "See, this is new"? It has already been in ancient times before us."

Ecclesiastes 1: 9b & 10

*T*hough only recently gaining media attention and wide-spread public awareness in our modern Christian society, Faith-Based Investing is, by a long shot, nothing new. In the grand sense of life and creation I would assert that since the beginning of time the concepts that are the foundations of Investing with Biblical Integrity have been evident and proclaimed in the principles and values illustrated throughout the Bible.

Some would say that would be a stretch, but is it? If, as a Christian, one's moral compass is set by God's word and God's word has been with us orally since He walked with Adam in the garden and textually since Moses began writing them down, one would have to agree that such foundations have truly been with us since the beginning.

Most people however would consider the application directly to stocks, bonds, and other investments a fairly new phenomenon starting as recently as the early 1990's. It was during this period that financial products and services expanded greatly with the explosive development of packaged investment products, mammoth increase in distribution channels, and massive marketing. Not until this time had there been any substantial Christian organized movement or Bible based investment organization to help those who so desired to invest with Biblical integrity.

It is also no coincidence that the internet had become widely available and information previously available only through painstaking and expensive research by private firms and educational institutes became available to the masses. This previously unparalleled access to information and communication allowed the rich and poor alike the ability to, with a click of the mouse, break through the fog and barriers to information that kept them in the dark for so long, realizing in seconds and minutes what was nearly impossible to know previously. It is easy to see why faith-based investing grew in exponential leaps at that time and why many believe that was the start of the faith based investing movement.

However, there is evidence that it began years earlier, in the 60's. It was during this time that Christians began looking at social issues and injustices, such as tobacco, apartheid, alcohol, and other human rights as is illustrated in this headline in the business and finance section of the New York Times in 1962;

"FAITH CRUSADE URGED; PEALS CALLS CHRISTIAN SOCIAL ISSUES PARAMOUNT NOW"[3]

It was a time of rethinking and questioning life decisions, including financial activities and the impact of those decisions on the American culture, the world, and personal contentment. The telephone and the television had matured and become common and widely used. The farm was no longer disconnected from the city or the world for that matter. Nightly news was distributed throughout America. Suffering in far-away lands, discrimination at home, political dishonesty, war and corporate corruption

---

[3] "FAITH CRUSADE URGED; PEALS CALLS CHRISTIAN SOCIAL ISSUES PARAMOUNT" NOW FEBRUARY 5, 1962, MONDAY NEW YORK TIMES – SECTION: BUSINESS & FINANCE, PAGE 46, 164 WORDS

were now beginning to be brought under public scrutiny. It affected Christians and non-Christians alike.

During this period other organizations, seeing the influence Christian affinity groups could yield with their investment dollars, got on board with their own perspective and socially causes. Many of these other causes were unfortunately in direct opposition to the Christian worldview. It is this secular world view of affinity group investing that made the headlines and brought the concept of aligning personal values with investments to the social forefront during our lifetime. Social Responsible Investing or SRI, as it came to be known, became a valid and accepted criterion for investing. So much so that investment companies began catering directly to these groups. It became evident that personal beliefs, including morals, Biblical or otherwise, could be and were a strong influence in the investment decision making process.

The same attention, and sadly the same personal desire, was not mainstreamed till many years later for the Christian Worldview investor. Without a doubt there have always been Christian individuals who have questioned the sanity and morality of aligning themselves, through their investments, with companies blatantly offensive to their Christian beliefs but the era of mass communication, made possible by television and the telephone, brought light to issues that for many were hidden in darkness.

Yet long before technology could illuminate issues of moral concern for investors were available or even conceived, the issues themselves and the desire to avoid being a participant thereof, was alive and well. There is evidence that the concept of Faith-Based Investing started long before the 1990's or the 1960's for that matter. In fact, two hundred years ago John Wesley's sermon on the Use of Money proclaimed:

> "But this it is certain we ought not to do; we ought not to gain money at the expense of life... [Those] who have anything to do with taverns, [brothels]... If they are either sinful in themselves, or natural outlets to sin of various kinds, then, it is to be feared, you have a sad account to make."

> —John Wesley, The Use of Money

In this single thought John Wesley clearly identified and defined the foundational concept of faith-based investing. It is to avoid the personal gain from (exploitation of) and the financial bonding to businesses that produce, promote, and profit from sinful activity including but not limited to abortion, alcohol and prostitution.

Without a doubt these Biblical directives for Faith Based Investing were clearly understood in his time. It also seems evident, from Christian literature of that era, that the Christian character to follow those directives, for those few who had the means to invest, was strong indeed. Possibly much stronger than today. Yet even this was not the beginning of Faith Based Investing.

We can travel back even further, another 200 years, to the early-mid 16th century. It is at this time in history the French theologian and pastor John Calvin stating the positive position of a faith-based decision process over our assets (investments).

> "In regard to everything that God has bestowed upon us, and by which we can aid our neighbor, we are his stewards, and are bound to give an account of our stewardship: moreover, that the only right mode of administration is that which is regulated by love."

> —John Calvin, The Life of a Christian

His declaration was and is to manage (administer) our investments in and through the guidelines of love. Defined by the context of this quote the definition of love would include love for our neighbor and the love of God. Though I do not believe there are many who would try to invoke or impose on this definition an opposing concept, to be sure, I will state without reserve the focus or source of love here would exclude the love of money.

A look at the Biblical explanation of love might help to understand this quote more fully.

> "Love suffers long and is kind; love does not envy; love does not parade itself, is not puffed up; does not behave rudely, does not seek its own, is not provoked, thinks no evil; does not rejoice in iniquity, but rejoices in the truth; bears all things, believes all things, hopes all things, endures all things."
>
> —I Corinthians 13:4-7

It is in the light of this guiding principle that John Calvin instructs us on how to execute Biblical stewardship over "everything" bestowed upon us by God. Everything excludes nothing and includes investments. We are instructed to keep our investment activities within the guidelines of love, participating only in those things that do not provoke, act rudely, rejoice in iniquity, or think evil, to invest only in that which does not harm others or ourselves. To bring this back to today and possibly help in the development of your own faith-based investing policies you might ask yourself; "How could partnering with companies that use or abuse people ever reconcile with these tenets of love?"

But wait, we have not yet reached the earliest evidence of Faith Based Investing. Let us jump back in time still another hundred years to the mid 1500's and listen to what Martin Luther had to say about those who profit from Biblically offensive business activities.

> "Among themselves the merchants have a common rule which is their chief maxim... I care nothing about my neighbor; so long as I have my profit and satisfy my greed, of what concern is it to me if it injures my neighbor in 10 ways at once? There you see how shamelessly this flies squarely in the face not only of Christian love but also of natural law."
>
> —Martin Luther, 1524

Wow. Could it be stated any more firmly? Shame, he says, shame on those who use or abuse others for profit. Could this include such activities as prostitution and pornography? Could it also include child labor, slavery, and other oppressive and abusive worker practices? What about the manufacturing and promotion of addictive products, products that harm the consumer? How about companies with polluted, unsafe, and unhealthy working conditions? Such attitudes and actions are not only void of Christian love but are a flagrant opponent to such doctrine.

It is evident that Martin Luther, John Calvin and John Wesley as well as many other Biblical scholars of old, had no problem realizing the Biblical directives of money and investments. Their writings help clarify and cement the understanding that Faith-Based Investing precepts are and have been common throughout the history of the church. It is not a new revelation to today's generation of Christians.

Why then does it seem so new and amazing? What has changed or happened to bring illumination to such a time cured concept?

It was not too long ago that only a small portion of Americans had any exposure, outside of their pension statements, to the investment world.

"In 1954 the Dow Jones Industrial Average high was 381.17. Today the Dow Jones stands more than 26 times higher than it did then. In 1954 there were 115 mutual funds in operation in this country, with investments worth $6.1 billion. In 2002 the number was more than 10,000 mutual funds controlling $7 trillion in capital. The percentage of people owning stocks and mutual funds has grown explosively as well, with over half the population directly holding financial securities. Many more have interests in pension funds."[4]

It is estimated that in 1960 only about 15% of American households owned stocks or stock mutual funds directly. Then the world changed. Companies and government started moving the responsibility of retirement to the individual. Thus, the advent of IRA's in the 1970's and the explosion of mutual funds through the 1980's and 1990's as well as the transition of many companies from company managed retirement plans to self-managed 401k's. Over a very short span of time the stock market became as common as the supermarket to Middle America. The widespread prosperity that quickly followed World War II to present and the media explosion that accompanied the ever increase in personal wealth, all came together in moving the mass of America from investment window shopping to reality. Could it be that as the investment arena has been embraced by the masses, so has the need to consider what and how we invest?

Could it also be possible that as Christians, as we individually and collectively grow in Christ, truth and relevance of our actions are ever more being revealed by our God and Savior? And to that extent what seemed

---

[4] THE 50 BIGGEST CHANGES IN THE LAST 50 YEARS BY JOHN STEELE GORDON – THE AMERICAN HERITAGE MAGAZINE JUNE/ JULY 2004 VOLUME 55, ISSUE 3

unimportant yesterday is illuminated by His perfect light for what it truly is today. Each on their path of sanctification. Each growing sensitive to His righteousness, in His time. Each sharing what they have gleaned in their journey toward perfection.

I would like to share a quote that influenced my life in general and guided my path as a Financial Advisor. One that punctuates the importance and history of Biblically Responsible Investing. I pray it will be impactful in your life as you continue to discern God's will for your investments.

> "A free Christian should act from within with a total disregard for the opinions of others. If a course is right, he should take it because it is right, not because he is afraid not to take it. And if it is wrong, he should avoid it though he lose every earthly treasure and even his very life as a consequence."

— A. W. Tozer (1897-1963)

Lessons Learned

---•---

Humble Revelations for Your Consideration

There are those who say the Bible can be interpreted any way a person wants to interpret it. That is true. Any book can be interpreted any way a person choses. Yet, that does not intimate the true meaning of the author is being respected. Is it possible that we twist and bend God's intent to fit our personal desires? The reasons could vary why one would do so. It could be outright rejection and rebellion of God or possibly simply due to the lack of faith we have in God's perfect plans for our life. Maybe it could be a lack of understanding, bad teaching, or even that God may have of yet given one the discernment of certain portions of His word. My experience has lead me to believe that as one grows in their faith of Christ the clearer the meaning and intent of His word becomes. This is evidenced in those times that God illuminated, gave me understanding, regarding His word, that not so long before I had struggled to understand.

It does seem true that each of us, seeking an ever deeper relationship with God, receives understanding of varying degrees at differing times in our life. No two journeys, lives, are exactly the same. As such I cannot tell you, outside of God's word, what may be true and what you need to do. I can only share what I believe God has revealed to me. It is then between you and Him to discern what is truth and of value and where this foolish man has gotten in the way and inserted that of his own understanding.

So, if I may, please let me share what the path of investing with Biblical integrity has convicted in me.

First, as a Christian, I am to be aware, awake, and conscious of what I do with my life and live it on purpose.

1 Corinthians 15:34 (NKJV) Awake to righteousness, and do not sin;...

And to care for my neighbor, put others before myself, turn away from sin and separate myself from those that embrace sin including sexual immorality, drunkenness, greed, laziness, gluttony, murder, stealing....

Ephesians 5:11 (NKJV) And have no fellowship with the unfruitful works of darkness, but rather expose *them*.

I am to be careful not to put myself in a relationship with those who don't hold the same values God has instilled in me. Especially one where I have little or no control.

2 Corinthians 6:14 (NKJV) Do not be unequally yoked together with unbelievers. For what fellowship has righteousness with lawlessness? And what communion has light with darkness?

Psalms 1:1 (NKJV) Blessed is the man ... Who walks not in the counsel of the ungodly, Nor stands in the path of sinners, Nor sits in the seat of the scornful;

His desire is that I embrace the example of His love and put behind me the misguided values of my life before Christ.

1 Peter 1:13-16 (NKJV) Therefore gird up the loins of your mind, be sober, and rest your hope fully upon the grace that is to be brought to you at the revelation of Jesus Christ; as obedient children, not conforming yourselves to the former lusts, as in your ignorance; but as He who called you is holy, you also be holy in all your conduct, because it is written, "Be holy, for I am holy."

And in everything I do, glorify God.

1 Corinthians 10:31 (NKJV) Therefore, whether you eat or drink, or whatever you do, do all to the glory of God.

And that is why the knowledge of Investment Stewardship is important. Because in the Bible God commands me:

1 Corinthians 15:33-34 (NKJV)Do not be deceived: "Evil company corrupts good habits." Awake to righteousness, and do not sin;

The bottom line? By owning stocks that produce, provide, or promote Biblically offensive activities I would, through my ownership, become a participant in these sinful activities. If these activities cause others to stumble, I as a stock owner of that company am partially responsible for initiating such stumbling. If the companies value increases because my stock purchase, and that of others, bid the stock up then we have contributed to the growth of a company that is offending God. If such companies give financial donations to organizations involved in Biblically offensive activities I have participated in funding the enemies of God.

Why is investing with Biblically integrity important? Because I am commanded by God to sin no more and my stock ownership could unequally yoke me to the corporate sin of the company I have purchased ownership in.

If my life as a Christian is to be honoring to God, then my actions cannot compromise that objective. I personally have come to a point in my life where I realize ever action is either an act of worship or an act of rebellion against the one true God. This includes my actions regarding money, possessions, and investments.

Solutions

———————— ❖ ————————

Matthew's Two-Part Process

*W*hat solutions are there for those who wish to honor God with their investments? Though still somewhat limited there are resources, products and professionals available today, that were scarce not so many years ago to help you. (I have included a list of resources and links for your use in the back of this book.) These resources and guidance can help make it possible to invest with integrity.

Developing a plan is always a good starting point. To begin developing your own investment plan consider utilizing the two-part process, inspired by Matthew 10:16 that has from the beginning been the foundational guideline at Integrity Investors, LLC, for our multidiscipline approach to investment management.

Matthew 10:16(NKJV) Behold I send you forth as sheep in the midst of wolves: be ye therefore wise as serpents and harmless as doves.

The Greek word for "wise" in this verse is the word "phronimos", meaning prudent, mindful of one's interest. The word "harmless" is the Greek word "akeraios", meaning without a mixture of evil, free from guile, innocent, simple.

If we are only harmless as a dove we may very well get eaten alive by the wolves of the world. If we are only wise as a serpent then we may end up hurting others. The key I find in these verses is to embrace both in our lives. We need the tools and wisdom to understand how to develop a portfolio, to pick investments that correlate with our objectives, personality and time horizons. We need knowledge and understanding of how the stock market and bond market works, how to analyze and research investments, how to define and manage risk and how to develop an investment discipline. This utilization of worldly knowledge, understanding how money works, is the "being wise as a serpent" part of the formula.

We also need to be aware of the impact our investments have in our lives and the lives of others. By being conscious of what we are participating in and supporting with our investment dollars we can purposely choose investment products that do not compromise our personal beliefs and that do not harm others. Utilizing care and compassion in the use of our worldly wisdom is "being harmless as a dove"

Investing with integrity means your money works to achieve both of these distinct yet highly compatible objectives. Your money can be put to work on achieving your personal financial objectives such as creating a secure and comfortable future for yourself, caring for and educating your family, and all important financial objective you may have, while deliberately utilizing only investment products that are in alignment with your beliefs. A Biblically Responsible approach to investing helps your money perform both tasks without compromise. You can invest with biblical integrity.

The Process – Discernment

> "Test all things; hold fast what is good. Abstain from every form of evil."
>
> 1 Thessalonians 5:21-22

How do individuals "abstain from every form of evil" regarding their investments? What strategies could be utilized?

The most utilized process is called screening. An investor can do this by either participating in investments that promote positive Biblical values (positive screening) or by avoiding those investments that participate in activities that they believe would be offensive to God (negative screening). Both are valid methods and though negative screens have dominated the Biblically Responsible Investment arena, we are seeing more and more positive screening being used, as well as a combination of both.

Someone who wishes to use "positive screening" as part of their investments selection criteria would start by composing a list of measurable "positive" attributes of companies that demonstrate values and actions they believe are in alignment with their Biblical principles. The attributes on this list would need to be observable and/or measurable, otherwise it would be impossible to discern whether a company possesses the right stuff to be an investment candidate. Some attributes that might be used in a Christian-Based "positive" screen process could include how a company;

- Cares for their employees by paying fair and respectable wages.

- Respects their vendors by paying their bills as promised.

- Serves their clients by delivering products and services that actually do what they advertised they would do.

- Honors their stockholders by honest accounting and responsible corporate stewardship.

- Illustrates proper discernment in what, where and how it participates in charitable events and giving.

- Creates products and services, that promote and increase healthy and productive lifestyles.

A "positive" screening methodology would then utilize a list similar to the previous defined positive attributes to sort through the maze of companies available and identify those companies that demonstrate these attributes as potential investments and eliminate those that don't. The final step would be to evaluate the financial qualities of the stocks that passed the positive screening process for possible inclusion in their portfolio.

A similar process would be used by those who would use a "negative" screening methodology. One who desires to utilize "negative" screening would begin by defining the "negative" attributes of companies that demonstrate values and actions they believe are in conflict with their Biblical principles. Just like "positive" screening the attributes on this list would need to be observable and/or measurable, otherwise it would be impossible to discern whether a company, by its activities, eliminates itself from being an investment candidate. Such definable activities could include;

- The use and abuse of individuals for sexual activities such as pornography and prostitution.

- Abortion-including the production and distribution of abortifacients.

- The production and promotion of products and services that harm or even destroy the consumer. This could include alcohol, tobacco, drugs, and gambling as well as any other addictive products and services.

- Entertainment and publication that promote, desensitize and program our society to reject God and the Bible.

- Human trafficking.

- Additionally, screens for some may include:
  - Abusive labor practices.
  - Abusive environmental activities.

A negative screening approach to investing would strive to eliminate companies based on their negative activities, leaving a pool of investments that could then be evaluated for their financial possibilities. It is important to understand that negative screens are as valid and useful as positive screens.

Both screening processes can produce informative insights that may help you to invest more purposefully. Many of today's professional money managers with a desire to invest with Biblical integrity utilize both.

Decide who will manage your portfolio

—————————❖—————————

If you prefer to do it yourself

*I*f you prefer making and managing your own investments, there are certain resources and processes you may want to consider. First, to be wise as a serpent, as discussed in the previous pages, begin by defining your investment selection criteria. I believe that successful investing requires, at the very least a buy-sell discipline. That is, a planned purchase criterion and exit strategy for your stocks or any other investment selection. When selecting investments to purchase, even the most flippant investor has some sort of criteria. It may be as simple as past performance or because their uncle purchased it, or it could be based on complicated technical and fundamental research including PE and other ratios, momentum, relative strength calculations, etc. The point is that most investors have criteria, valid or not, they use to select stocks. I believe the intelligent investor understands, at a minimum, three things.

1. The primary goal they desire to achieve through investing

2. What type of investment product(s) are best suited for that goal

3. The primary risks and limitations associated with such investments.

Beyond that, the paths of portfolio development are many and the theories plentiful. Open any investment magazine and I am sure will find articles in abundance encompassing multiple investment management styles. Search the internet and millions of systems, thousands of tutorials, and limitless opinions are available to help you be a better investor, to become "wise as serpent", and to gain worldly knowledge of investment management. It can be complicated and confusing, overwhelming or oversimplified depending on who you read or listen to.

However, when it comes to investment portfolio development I would like to share just a couple of words of wisdom for your consideration.

The first tidbit is more a warning, than anything else, regarding predicting the future. If we trust the Bible, then we know only God can see the future. So beware of those in the world who claim to have a "system" or strategy that can tell you what will happen when, sometime in the future. This should include both buying and selling decisions.

On the other hand, God has given us the intelligence to understand the times. To be able to look at what is happening around us, be able to interpret the current conditions and act accordingly. Consider developing at least a basic understanding of fundamental and technical indicators. Find the ones that help you discern attributes of investments that you lean towards and then utilize these indicators to develop a buy-sell discipline for your investments. Consider developing a system that guides your decision process so emotions don't hijack your investment decisions.

Finally, try to manage from a place of peace.... avoiding fear and greed. Emotions are the number one enemy to investing. Fear and greed, if left unchecked, will dictate your buy-sell decisions. Usually with devastating consequences. So much so that there is a technical indicator some professional investors use to determine when to get in or out of the market.

Consider the "small investors syndrome". The premise is small investors are guided by emotions. So when a stock or market starts going up, the small investors, out of fear don't jump in. Instead they watch the markets rise and rise. They stay on the sidelines, out of fear, knowing the market won't continue its run and afraid they would lose their money if they jumped in. Frustration grows as the market climbs day after day until they can't take it any longer. Greed takes over and they finally jump in. Unfortunately for them they waited until much of the run was over and, in effect, bought in at the top.

Of course, at this point, the market turns and begins to drop. The small investors can't believe it. They see their loses but need to believe that the market will correct itself any time now. Anyway, it's just a paper loss unless he sells….right? Each dip in the market is like a smack in the face to the small investor. They just can't accept the loss, greed keeps them hanging on hoping to at least get back to breakeven. Then fear of losing it all takes over and the small investor is unable to stay the course and sells everything…….at the bottom.

By measuring smaller trades in the stock market, a manager can get indicators of what the small investor is doing and use this as just one more gauge of tops and bottoms of the market. The way the professional investor plays this is to do just the opposite of what the small investor, led by fear and greed, does.

Developing a system of rules based on technical and fundamental indicators, testing these rules and sticking to them restrains the emotions of investing. At Integrity Investors, LLC we have devised such a discipline. We call it the Integrity BFT Analysis. (Biblical, Fundamental and Technical Analysis).

The Biblical analysis, of Integrity Investors BFT Analysis, determines if a company's activities are in alignment or contrast with Biblical values. The fundamental analysis reveals the financial strengths and weaknesses of a company and the technical analysis reveals how a company performs under different market conditions and competitive environments. A simple way to look at this is that "Biblical" determines who we will consider, "Fundamental" determines which of those "Biblical" companies to buy and "Technical" determines when to buy and sell.

It would be easy, at this point, to deviate away from the faith-based focus of this writing to discuss the "wise as a serpent" portion of investing. Yet, there are endless books already written on this topic and so little written on the faith-based portion. So instead of 400 pages on how the stock and bond markets work, stock picking risks, management strategies, etc. I have included several book titles and websites dealing specifically with the "wise as a serpent" portfolio strategies at the back of this book that I believe may be relevant in your pursuit of worldly investment knowledge. See "Recommended Resources".

For now, let's stay on track with our faith based discussion which leads us to the second part of our "Serpent and Dove" philosophy.

Along with the technical and fundamental investment resources an informed investor would use to evaluate markets and investments, please consider the following resources to help you with your Biblical Responsible analysis.

• <u>More Than Money Ministries</u> – A nonprofit organization with a special focus on Investment Stewardship. This site has a bunch of BRI materials to help you with your decisions. They also provide a free screening service for individuals and have newsletters and blogs highlighting investment concepts. More Than Money's "Shining the light on Wall Street" segment is a research concept that digs deep into both the good and the bad of publicly traded companies. <u>www.mtmministries.org</u>

• <u>Evaluator Services</u> – This is the Biblically Responsible data provider for investment professionals. The good news is they will screen individual investor portfolios for you for free, no strings attached. <u>www.evalueator.com</u>

- <u>The National Association of Christian Financial Consultants (NACFC)</u> – The first organization formed to teach, train and encourage Christian financial professionals to provide "Biblical Responsible Investing to their clients." You can find resources and professionals committed to BRI here. <u>www.nacfc.org</u>

- <u>Kingdom Advisors</u> – Kingdom Advisors provides advocacy, training, and community for financial professionals who are specialists in offering biblically wise advice. Though Their focus is primarily on Christian Financial Planning, their BRI affinity group has been growing steadily. It is a great resource to find stewardship training and Christian professionals. <u>www.kingdomavdisors.com</u>.

Using Professional Money Management

If you decide you prefer the benefits of a professional investment advisor consider the following criteria in your selection process.

- ***First and foremost – Seek out an advisor who embraces your Biblical values.*** This is critical. If the person you are turning to for financial advice regarding the blessings God has entrusted to you, does not believe in the foundations of your stewardship, how can they even begin to counsel you in fulfilling those beliefs? Where would their advice be coming from and how often might it conflict with your Biblical values?

- *Seek out an advisor who understands God's Word on financial stewardship*, one that shows competence and acceptance of Biblically Responsible Investment concepts. Not everyone who claims Christ is studied in the ways of Biblical Stewardship. As such it is important to determine the commitment and depth of knowledge your possible investment advisor has concerning Biblical wisdom regarding money, possessions and investments. One way to do this is to look for advisors who hold a respected designation in such studies. Three such designation are listed here.

  o <u>The CFCA designation</u> is one such designation. It is earned and administered through the National Association of Christian Financial Consultants and was the first professional designation for Christian investment advisors in the investment industry.

o <u>The CKA, Kingdom Advisor</u>, designation is earned and administered through Kingdom Advisors.

o <u>The BRIQ</u>, Biblically Responsible Investing Qualified seal can only be used by investment advisors who meet the strict standards of More Than Money Ministries. To be BRI Qualified an investment professional must meet the following standards.

1. Be licensed and in good standing with the national and state governing bodies.

2. Show competence and acceptance of Biblically Responsible Investment concepts. The designation program from the NACFC is one of the ways an investment professional can demonstrate such competency.

3. Have proof of resources necessary to perform BRI analysis. This would include access to screening services that meet strict BRI guidelines and access to products and services that comply with BRI criteria.

4. A profession of faith in Jesus Christ as their savior and the Bible as the inerrant written word of God.

5. Is a participant and is in good standing with their local church.

- *Look for other Credentials.* There are many designations and certifications an advisor can have including the more familiar CFP, CFA, CPA, CFS, and ChFC designations. An advisor who earns and maintains such credentials shows a commitment to an advanced degree of worldly knowledge beyond government licensing as well as committing to high ethical standards. A combination of these "secular" designations with one of the Biblically based designations would indicate the advisor has studied to gain the knowledge necessary to address both the serpent and dove aspects of a Biblically grounded investment plan described earlier in this chapter.

- *Consider the length of time the advisor and the their firm* have they been in practice. Longevity often can equate to experience and wisdom. It can also show a commitment to the investment discipline.

- *Understand how your advisor is paid.* Will your advisors and their firm make commissions on the buying and selling of products or will they charge a fee for their services, or both? The difference not only affects costs but the standards an advisor is held to. In a perfect world, this would not be an issue. Unfortunately, we live in a fallen world and it is important to know what motivates and encourages your advisor's guidance.

Commission based advisors must only suggest investments that they believe are in alignment with your goals, needs and unique situation. This is called the suitability standard. A fee-based advisor is held to what many consider a higher "fiduciary" standard. This requires the advisor to put your best interest above their own at all times.

Of course, it is important to know what charges will be, whether commissioned or fee-based. You should be comfortable asking up front for a breakdown of account charges, trade fees, miscellaneous charges as well as a commissions schedule. This is common practice for advisors to provide such information.

With commissions, it is also important to understand the turnover rate of your advisor's portfolio. The more turnover the more commissions. This doesn't mean buying and selling is bad, it just means there are commission cost associated in doing so along with the normal transaction fees. You might ask how this affects the advisor's recommendations on buying and selling.

With fee-based agreements, the turnover rate is considerably less important from a cost perspective, since no commissions are collected on the trades. The fee-based advisor plans usually fall into one of three different billing models.

1. Assets Under Management Billing is the most common. You are billed based on a percentage of assets the advisor manages for you. The percentage usually goes down as the amount of assets increases.

2. Hourly Fee. You are billed based on the amount of time they spend with you and working on your portfolio or planning projects.

3. Flat fee or fixed fee. You are billed based on a predetermined fee for desired services and management.

- ***Consider what additional services the advisor provides.*** Most investment firms offer help with goal planning, retirement, educational, full financial and estate planning as either additional services or integrated into their investment services. This makes sense as it is important for them to understand what and why you are investing, who you are and what is important to you to be able to manage your portfolio in alignment with the uniqueness of your life. Consider what services are important to you and find someone who fits your needs.

- *Ethics and standing.* How do you know if your potential investment advisor has had or is having ethical or legal problems? It is easy to check. Just go to https://brokercheck.finra.org/, a website created by FINRA, the governing authority over investment professionals. It is simple, quick and easy to navigate and will give you a snapshot of a broker's employment history, licensing information and regulatory actions, arbitrations and complaints.

- *Prayer.* I know it goes without saying, for those who have a personal relationship with the one true God. Yet I want to encourage you anyway. No matter what information is available, how perfect everything may seem, God's insights include far more information, including the past present and future. Pray first that God will help you past yourself, your fears, greed, pride and insecurities. Then pray to trust His guidance and to give you clarity of His will, whatever that may be, for you. Then, when you are at total peace, make your decision and pray some more.

Before you Leave

———————————•———————————

I want to both congratulate and encourage you.

Congratulations!

. . . on taking the time to read about a topic and explore concepts that merge, what many would consider incompatible, the spiritual and the financial. Many, in their walk with God, come to the crossroads of belief, between the spiritual and the physical. Wanting more than this temporal physical world has to offer, some might consciously try to deny their place in the reality of the here and now to embrace the reality of the spiritual. Yet somewhere deep inside, most sense that there is a better solution. One that doesn't force us to deny the reality of the physical world for the spiritual, but embrace a greater reality. The reality of God that includes both. God's reality that born us into the physical and again into the spiritual. The all-encompassing reality of everything. No conflict, just alignment.

I pray you will welcome Investing with Biblical Integrity as an investment philosophy that embraces the need for real world results, while purposely choosing to invest without compromising your own moral beliefs. In doing so, you just might find more joy and peace in your life as you broaden your relationship with God to include your investment decisions. The more we embrace Christ, the source of all that it is good, the greater the opportunities to realize His joy and realize even more of His peace that surpasses all understanding.

Encouragement

Nothing happens on accident. Your reading of this had a purpose. Maybe someone recommended or gave it to you or maybe you picked it up on your own. No matter how it got in your hands, it was for a reason.

Is it possible that God has given you a desire to honor Him in all things, including your investments? Could this be a stepping stone, an encouragement to invest with Biblical integrity? Is it possible that after reading this book you are at least curious to see what Biblical conflicts may be in your portfolio?

I want to encourage you to explore, become conscious of how your investments are aligned. Whether you fully accept the concepts explored here or not, be curious and consider having your investments screened. You can do this on your own, through one of the websites mentioned earlier and in the Resource list at the back of this book, or with an advisor of your choice. Biblically Responsible Investment Advisors can be found by going to nacfc. com and mtmministries.com websites. I also want to encourage you to be at peace in your journey to invest with Biblical integrity. It is between you and God, and God loves you.

Recommended Resources

Books

Bible Based Books (Dove)

Money, Possessions, and Eternity by Randy Alcorn

Managing Gods Money by Randy Alcorn

The Treasure Principle by Randy Alcorn

Kingdom Gains by Dwight Short

Diamond of Life by Mick Owens

Your Money Counts by Howard Dayton

Debt Free Living by Larry Burkett

The Complete Guide to Managing Your Money by Larry Burkett

The New Master Your Money by Ron Blue

Never Enough by Ron Blue

I found Jesus In Stock Market by Cassandra Layman

The Pursuit of God by A. W. TOZER

The Fear of Money by Dan Celia

Profits or Principles by Dwight Short

Rich Christians in an Age of Hunger by Ronald Sider

The Bible Inc. by Michael Pink

Additional resources can be found at www. TheWallStreetAwakening.com/resources

Investment Concepts (Serpent)

The MisBehavior of Markets by Benoit Mandelbrot

Bull's Eye Investing by John Mauldin

Trend Following by Michael W. Covel

Way of the Turtle by Curtis M. Faith

High Probability Trading by Marcel Link

Stock Market Logic by Norman Fosback

Websites

Integrity Investors.com
www.integrityinvestors.com

More Than Money Ministries
www.mtmministries.org

eVALUEator.com
www.evalueator.com

NACFC
www.nacfc.org

The Timothy Plan
www.timothyplan.com

Eventide
www.eventide.com

Kingdom Advisors
www.kingdomadvisors.com

Eternal Perspective Ministries
www.epm.org

Investopedia
www.investopedia.com

Brokercheck
https://brokercheck.finra.org

BRIInstitute
www.briinstitute.com

ChristianPF
www.christianPF.com

Financial Issues Dan Celia
www.financialissues.org

Crosswalk.com
www. Crosswalk.com

Crown Financial Ministries
www.crown.org

Christian Investment Forum
https://christianinvestmentforum.org/

Additional resources can be found at
www.TheWallStreetAwakening.com/resources

About the Author

———◦———

Mark A. Minnella, CFS, CFCA, CKA

*A*s founder and President of Integrity Investors, LLC, Mark is passionate about treating his company as a ministry, enabling his clients to align their investments with their Christian values. In pursuit of that God-driven passion and to impact more than his own client base, Mark designed the first faith-based professional designation program in the industry, the CFCA offered through the National Association of Christian Financial Counselors, a ministry Mark co-founded with some of his fellow pioneers in Biblically Responsible investing. The portfolio management process used by Integrity Investors was born out of the need for excellence in money management with the requisite focus on stewardship of the Lord's resources. His growing client base and portfolio services offered through other Christian financial planners provides the platform for his ministry in the marketplace.

Mark was host of the radio show originally named "Financial Peace", which later changed the name to "More Than Money", for over 17 years, airing on the Bott radio network KSIV as well as KXEN and KJSL in St Louis. Through his radio program he was able to reach people with the message of stewardship, investing with Biblical integrity, and encouragement. Additionally, as a featured columnist for CBS MarketWatch, Money Talk, Mpower magazine, the Musicianary magazine, Metro Voice Christian newspaper and the Good News Herald, Mark has been recognized as a pioneer and expert in the Biblically Responsible Investment movement. His designations, licenses, and registrations have included CFCA Certified Christian Financial Consultant, CFS-Certified Funds Specialist, CKA, Certified Kingdom Advisor and NASD Series 7, 24, 63, 65.

Mark served on the board of directors for The Timothy Plan Family of Mutual Funds and was one of the founders and past president of the National Association of Christian Financial Consultants, Inc. and founder More Than Money ministries, a 501c3.

In 2014, Mark was honored with the Integrity Award which was established to recognize Christians whose actions and convictions have honored God in the process of promoting Biblical Investment Stewardship According to the National Association of Christian

Financial Consultants, Mark Minnella was chosen for his service, leadership and dedication to promoting and living the principles of Biblical Investment Stewardship.

Mark's greatest joy is his wife Cynthia, his three grown children, Mark, David and Michelle and his grandchildren. He is a Deacon at Bethel Community Church, in St Louis, MO, where he currently lives.

If you have questions for Mark or would like to book him for a speaking engagement or interview, please contact his office at;

314-212-1404
12647 Olive Blvd, Suite 105
Creve Coeur, MO 63141
mark@integrityinvestors.com

CPSIA information can be obtained
at www.ICGtesting.com
Printed in the USA
FFOW03n0917200618